A BETTER TODAY

Improve Your Life In 30 Days With This Fun, Inspirational & Motivational Challenge

DIANE FORSTER
2X Award Winning Life & Mindset Coach
Best Selling Author

Copyright 2021 Diane Forster
All Rights Reserved

ISBN: 979-87826744-8-9

Dedicated to my twins
Melanie and Robert
and to all who seek to find more
magic in their TODAY.

Acknowledgements

Thank you, Melanie D'Andrea and Robert D'Andrea, for your love and understanding that your momma marches to the beat of her own drummer. Sometimes a rebel, sometimes kooky, but always, always, always coming from love. You two are the most precious gifts in the world to me.

Thank you to the rest of my family…

My dad, Jack Forster, who loves me and encourages me. You're one of my biggest fans, and I'm truly grateful for you.

My sisters, Arlene Forster and Cheryl Smith. I love you both so much and I am so lucky and blessed to have you in my life.

To my mom in heaven, Rosann Joy Ranucci Forster, my angel and guide. Even though you are no longer in the physical, I am beyond blessed and lucky that I have the ability to hear you and see you. Thanks for always pointing me in the right direction.

To the team who helped create this book…

Sandi Masori, for helping me publish this book. Thank you for all your attention and guidance. You're amazing at what you do!

Kelly Delisle for helping me put all the pieces together and for always listening to my crazy stories with an open mind and open heart! Thank you for also seeing what's best for me when I was too close to it. My protector!

Acknowledgements

Brie Hancy for being a part of the creation of the original 30 day challenge video series and coming to work every day asking, "what's tomorrow's challenge?" Your excitement and support linger with me to this day!

Cherry Alongay, my new addition who's already a huge part of the team! Thank you for your hard work, excitement and enthusiasm.

Thank you to all my clients, fans and followers, who inspire me every day and catapult me forward to keep learning, growing and expanding so that I may serve you at the highest level possible.

Thank you to the communities that I belong to…Kim Walsh Phillips and Powerful Professionals Coaching, Bari Baumgardner and Blue Melnick and the entire team at SAGE Event Management and the LEAP community, Jen Gottlieb and Chris Winfield and the entire team and members at Super Connector, Coach Ron Tunick…my friend and mentor, and the entire Landing Big Whales Group. It's because of all of you bringing out the best of me. I have the best village ever!!!

Thank you for the incredible team of editors, graphic designers and formatters for making this book look great.

Last, a big thank you to you, the reader, for giving me a reason to create this book for you. Enjoy this journey and make sure you have fun!

Welcome to The 30 Day Challenge on How to Have "A Better TODAY!"

Are you ready? I use the word "challenge" loosely here. The truth of the matter is…this is going to be easy, fun and simple! As I've shared many times and I even talk about in my book, "I Have Today…Find Your Passion, Purpose and Smile…Finally!" when you do simple, easy things where you change, you break habits, you create new ones, you create new rituals, when you do them subtly, easy things like this that are easy to remember, they build upon each other, and that creates lasting, permanent, positive change.

There are 30 challenges in this book…one for each day. Read one challenge at a time, do that day's challenge, and recap what happened for you at the end of each day (or the next morning.). These are designed to fit into your life easily. Even though they are simple and easy, don't discount its power! I've been doing some of these every day for several years, and they have positively impacted my life. My hope is that they do the same thing for you!

Simple, simple, simple. We tend to make life so much more complicated than it is. This challenge is meant to bring more meaning, fun, joy and fulfillment to your life. Enjoy it!

Please note that this book is the transcription of a 30 day video series I created, and the transcription is in unedited conversational tone and format.

I'd love your feedback. Send me your comments at info@dianeforster.com.

If you'd like the video version of the challenge, register at www.abettertodaychallenge.com.

Please follow me and subscribe to my YouTube Channel, podcast, social media and check out my website. There are many ways to get your daily inspiration and help you live an inspired, intentional life.

To find me anywhere, use the links below:

dianeforster.com
facebook.com/DianeForsterOfficial
facebook.com/IHaveTodaywithDianeForster
instagram.com/DianeForsterOfficial
pinterest.com/dianeforsterofficial
twitter.com/dianefofficial
youtube.com/c/IHaveTodaywithDianeForster
linkedin.com/in/dianeforsterofficial/
clubhouse.com/@dianeforster

Okay…let's go!

With Love,
Diane

Table of Contents

Acknowledgements iv

Day 1   A Very Powerful Question 3
Day 2   When…Then 9
Day 3   Tell Three People Three Things 15
Day 4 $5.00 Can Make a Big Impact 21
Day 5   20 Things About Yourself 27
Day 6   Something Unexpected 33
Day 7   One Minute of Laughter 39
Day 8   Extra Time in Bed 45
Day 9   A Little Decadence 51
Day 10   An Unplanned Getaway 57
Day 11   The Power of the "Calm Alarm" 63
Day 12   A Taste of Something New 69
Day 13   A Road Never Traveled 75
Day 14   A Dozen Achieved Goals 81
Day 15   A Tiny Task to Tidy Up 87
Day 16   Music to Move You 93
Day 17   Don't "Should" All Over Yourself 99
Day 18   One Thing for Another 105

Table of Contents

Day 19	What's Your Wish, Wish, Wish	111
Day 20	Make Learning a Priority	117
Day 21	You Are a Magnet	123
Day 22	You Aren't Your Story	129
Day 23	Thirsty for Water	135
Day 24	Plant Power	141
Day 25	The Present of Presence	147
Day 26	Judgement Day…Not	153
Day 27	Worthy Words	159
Day 28	Decide to Decide	165
Day 29	Your Emails Can Wait	171
Day 30	Keep Your Feet on the Ground	177

In Gratitude	181
Now What?	183
About the Author	185

"A Better TODAY"

Day 1

A Very Powerful Question

I want you to say today, "Why does this day keep getting better and better?"

I want you to say it ALL day today, ALL DAY LONG!

"Why does this day keep getting better and better?" "Why does this day keep getting better and better?"

Set an alarm on your phone every hour if you need to. Write it down wherever you go. Just start repeating it over and over and watch the MIRACLES that start happening to you today! You'll notice all the subtle little things. Our miracles are big and small, so, at the end of the day, you're going to look back at your day and go "Wow, this day really DID get better and better!"

Where this comes from is a book I read by Noah St. John called "Afformations." We do afformations differently than we do affirmations. An afformation is simply putting the "why" word in front and posing our affirmations as a question instead of a statement. Because if we say affirmations and they don't resonate with us or we really don't believe it, our subconscious is going "Yeah, right." You're saying, "I am thin," or "I am wealthy," or whatever it is that you're trying to affirm, and there's a part of the brain that says, "No you're not" and "That's not true."

What happens with the "why" question is the subconscious goes to work on creating what you want to happen. It puts it in "action" mode. It's different than the "how" question. The "how" gets into logic, but the "why" helps it manifest into your life. If you haven't read that book, I highly recommend you get it. It's a great read!

I ask "why" questions a lot, but my favorite "why" question is "Why does this day keep getting better and better?"

That's my challenge to you. I want you to say that all day today, and I want to hear how this question, "Why does this day keep getting better and better?" has affected your life in a positive way.

A Very Powerful Question

RECAP YOUR DAY

Did you do the challenge?

What happened?

How was the experience?

"A Better TODAY"

Day 2

When...Then

It's Day 2 of our Challenge on How to Have a Better Today!

Yesterday's challenge, if you remember, was to ask yourself all day long, "Why does this day keep getting better and better?" I hope you saw improvement in your day yesterday using that question and try and plant that somewhere in the recesses of your mind and keep that "why" question active in your mind and active your life.

So, here we go with Challenge Number 2.

I want you to be aware of when you use "When/Then" statements. What I mean by that is a "When/Then" statement is something that implies,

"When I lose ten pounds, then I'll be happy."

"When I make a million dollars, then I can relax."

"When I'm X, then I'm Y."

Those are examples of "When/Then" statements. This dates back to when we were children, and our parents used this as an effective, simple instructional statement and a tool for getting their children to do something.

For example:

"When you put your shoes on, then we can go outside and play."

"When you eat the rest of your chicken, then you have more French fries." "When you brush your teeth, then I'll read you a story."

It's ingrained in our brain from childhood that when we do a certain act, then we'll get a reward. We grow up believing that we need certain situations and circumstances to create our happiness, and the truth of the matter is, that's just not the case.

It's an effective tool when parenting a child, but we grow up with that in our mind, thinking that circumstances need to be different than they are in order for us to be happy.

Therefore, I want you to be aware of when you're using "When/Then" statements and try and eliminate them out of your life. Because the truth is, when you do lose that weight, or when you do get that money, or you get that job, or you go on that trip…whatever happens in our lives, whatever goals that we have, that we strive for and work for…as soon as a goal is accomplished in our life, it's IMMEDIATELY replaced with another one!

That's just the way it is. I mean…that is just part of our journey and our path. It's never done, it's never over, and we're ever-expanding. There's always something else more to strive for, so be aware that "When/Then" will not create happiness.

You'll feel that momentary happiness when you reach it, but then, what comes into play is the "Now What" question. Let me explain…the reward or goal happens for you, and then you say, "Well, now what?"

There's sometimes even a level of disappointment after you achieve a goal, because it's been something that you've been striving for. So, the goal is to try and get the use of "When/Then" out of your life and realize that your happiness is a choice that you get to decide on RIGHT NOW.

That is my challenge for you for Day 2…is to try and be aware of those "When/Then" statements and try to eliminate them out of your life.

When...Then

RECAP YOUR DAY

Did you do the challenge?

_____
_____
_____
_____
_____

What happened?

_____
_____
_____
_____
_____

How was the experience?

_____
_____
_____
_____
_____

Day 3

Tell Three People Three Things

It is Day 3 of our 30 Day Challenge on How to Have a Better Today!

Day 1 was the "Why does this day keep getting better and better?" question.

Day 2 was to be aware of the "When/Then" statements and try to eliminate them out of your life.

Now, on Day 3, I'm going to make it easy for you to remember, because I'm all about making things easy for you.

Day 3 is going to involve you reaching out to three people and telling them three things. I want you to call three people and say, "I love you, I'm thinking about you, and I'm always here for you."

These are people that are special. They are not the people that you talk to on a regular basis. These are the people that…you know who these people are! These are the people that you should reach out to; you've been thinking about them. You know you should, but you just haven't, and the day gets away from you and you get busy. But you know that if you reach out to them, they are going to LIGHT UP when they hear from you! It's going to totally make their day which in turn is going to totally make your day that much better.

Remember, three people, tell them three things on day three: "I love you, I'm thinking about you, and I'm always here for you." That's it. I'm making it simple, simple, simple today.

Making these phone calls (you could text them if you want, but a phone call is so much better…and seeing them in person would be even better!) shouldn't take you more than 30 minutes out of your day…maybe an hour…but, what a gift you would be giving to these people and, in turn, to yourself.

That's it! Day 3, the challenge is reach to out to three people, tell them those three things: "I love you, I'm thinking about you, and I'm always here for you."

Have an amazing day. Be your magnificent selves.

RECAP YOUR DAY

Did you do the challenge?

What happened?

How was the experience?

"A Better TODAY"

Day 4

$5.00 Can Make a Big Impact

We're back with Day 4 of The 30 Day Challenge on How to Have a Better TODAY.

Day 1, we asked all day long, "Why does this day keep getting better and better?"

Day 2, we became aware of our use of "When/Then" statements.

Day 3, we contacted three people, told them three things: "I love you, I'm thinking about you, and I'm always here for you."

Day 4. What I want you to do today is I want you to give away $5.00. That's it! $5.00. You can give away more if you want to, but a minimum of $5.00.

We can all find $5.00. You could give it away to one person. You could give $1.00 to five people. You can gather all your loose change and disperse it out throughout the day to people you want to give it to. You could be at Starbucks buying coffee, and you could buy coffee for the person behind you. It doesn't matter how you do it but do some act of kindness where you're giving away a minimum of $5.00.

The reason why is, when we give like that, we get back tenfold! I'm not asking you to do it so that you get something in return. Just the act of giving, and putting it out there, is gift enough. You will see that it will come back to you in some crazy way. You're going to get some sort of refund check, or a credit on something, but somehow, you are going to get some monetary reward from it just by giving out the money.

I do it with money because everything is energy. Money is energy. In fact, 95% of money is electronic and digital. It's not even in paper form, coin form…physical form. It's actually REALLY energy exchanging.

It just feels SO GOOD to give. It does have a ripple effect, and when you give you will receive, but others will give as well. It just spreads the good feelings of giving just to give, just to be kind.

That's my challenge today. Really easy. Like I said, this is hardly a challenge these 30 days, but I'm trying to make it fun for you. It's to just create awareness of getting out of yourself and giving to somebody merely for the random act of kindness of giving.

$5.00 Can Make a Big Impact

RECAP YOUR DAY

Did you do the challenge?

What happened?

How was the experience?

"A Better TODAY"

Day 5

20 Things About Yourself

It's Day 5 of our 30 Day Challenge on How to Have a Better TODAY.

I'm going to recap again.

Day 1 started with saying asking all day long, "Why does this day keep getting better and better?"

Day 2 was being aware of our use of "When/Then' statements.

Day 3 was contacting three people and telling them those three things: "I love you, I'm thinking about you, and I'm always here for you."

Day 4 was to give away a minimum of $5.00.

Okay…Today, Day 5, here's your challenge.

I want you to write down 20 things that you like about yourself. That could be I'm a great mom. I'm really creative. I love my hair. I like jazz. Anything about yourself that you like, but 20 things.

Just a list of 20 things that are all positive things that you like about yourself. Then, what I want you to do with that list is stick it somewhere visible. Maybe it's on your nightstand, or on your desk at work, or on the vanity in the bathroom area, but put it someplace where you can see that list every single day and read that list.

Just appreciate yourself. Appreciate the things that you like about yourself. Hey, if you want to write more than 20 that's great but start with a list of 20 things that you really like about yourself.

The reason why I'm having you do that is when we look at the gifts and the things that we like about ourselves, that expands. Then, we see those things in other people, and "like attracts like."

It's a simple thing, but it's just another way to love yourself and nurture yourself more. Write that list of 20 things. I keep mine in my journal as my bookmark, and it keeps my place in my journal. So, every day when I write in my journal and I open it up, it's the first thing I see is that list of 20 things that I really like about myself.

Things like I'm a mother of twins (I'm really proud of that), I'm a sister, I'm an inventor, I love the beach, etc. Just simple, simple things like that that I just love and appreciate about myself.

Simple, simple like I told you. This is hardly a challenge!

RECAP YOUR DAY

Did you do the challenge?

What happened?

How was the experience?

"A Better TODAY"

Day 6

Something Unexpected

Day 6 of our 30 Day Challenge on How to Have a Better TODAY and I hope you're enjoying this because I'm having a lot of fun with this!

Okay, quick, quick recap.

Day 1: "Why does this day keep getting better and better?"

Day 2: Awareness of the "When/Then" statements.

Day 3: Tell three people those three things…"I Love You, I'm thinking about you, and I'm always here for you."

Day 4: Give away a minimum of $5.00.

Day 5: Write a list of 20 things that you like about yourself.

Okay, Day 6 is going to be fun!

Who doesn't love a surprise? Something nice? Something fun?

What I want you to do today is do something unexpected for one person.

Buy them flowers, send them a card, get them a gift, or take them somewhere. Take them out to dinner, or to a play, or something that you know that they would really enjoy. Do something unexpected for one person today. Just because! Just because you like them or love them. You care about them and you're thinking about them.

That's it. Couldn't it be any simpler than that?! Just do one unexpected thing. I use the word "gift" a lot because I see the gift in EVERY SINGLE THING that's happened in my life. I wasn't always that way, but I am this way now. Everything that I'm talking to you about comes from a place of experiencing and creating "gifts" in your life because LIFE itself is such a gift!

That's where it comes from. I get such a gift by doing these things for other people. There's such a gift in that, and you'll experience it as well. When you're doing for others and you get out of your head, you're putting your focus and emphasis on somebody else, which is so rewarding, and it does come back to YOU in so many wonderful ways.

That's what I want you to do today. Very simple, again just do something unexpected for someone and really make their day.

Something Unexpected

RECAP YOUR DAY

Did you do the challenge?

_____
_____
_____
_____

What happened?

_____
_____
_____
_____

How was the experience?

_____
_____
_____
_____

"A Better TODAY"

Day 7

One Minute of Laughter

Okay, we're one week into this challenge. This is so much fun! I think this day might be the most fun challenge so far.

What I'm doing is I'm going to recap each week. Then, starting next week on Day 8, I'll go through the next week and recap it for you. I'm going to recap Day 1 through 7 for you. The reason why I do that is because it's in the repetition that we remember. If I'm repeating it every day, I'm ingraining it in your brain so it will STICK. That is the reason why I'm doing it like this.

Day 1, remember, "Why does this day keep getting better and better?" I hope you continue to ask yourself that question.

Day 2, be aware of your "When/Then" statements.

Day 3, contact three people, tell them the three things: "I love you, I'm thinking about you, and I'm always here for you."

Day 4 was to give away $5.00.

Day 5 was to write a list of 20 things that you like about yourself.

Day 6 was to do an unexpected thing for one person.

Day 7, Here we go! I'm laughing already! I want you to spend one minute today, 60 seconds, laughing out loud!

Do you ever notice that if you see people laughing, you can't help but smile, and you begin to start laughing too? Especially if they're laughing hysterically, and they really get going. The momentum gets stronger, and the next thing you know they're snorting and making other noises! The laughter just builds and builds on it.

If you force yourself to laugh, what's going to happen is, after a couple of seconds, you're ACTUALLY going to be laughing!

Here's what I would do. I would go into a public place, like a park, or sit outside at a café or someplace similar. If you're alone by yourself, hold up your phone and pretend like you're talking to someone. Otherwise, people will think you're crazy if you're just sitting there by yourself laughing. But, let it go and just laugh out loud for a full minute!

First of all, that's so healthy and healing! We should be laughing every single day. Laughter truly is the best medicine, number one. Number two, it makes other people laugh. It's infectious and contagious! Have you ever noticed that? If you could see me right now, you would see that I can't wipe the smile off my face just thinking about it! We should all be laughing every single day (AT LEAST 60 seconds) of our life. I'm telling you; it would add years to our lives and a whole lot more happiness.

What I want to say about it is this…have you ever noticed someone walking down the street just laughing? Sometimes people walk by people laughing and you can tell what they are thinking by their expression, "Oh that person's insane." However, if you saw somebody crying, you instinctively have sympathy for that person. You feel bad for them, and your natural inclination is to feel sympathy, and to want to help. The laughter should be the thing that we're more attracted to. That's the thing that we should resonate more towards because it's so positive and uplifting.

If you feel weird about it, do it at home. If you're home alone, that's great. If somebody else is around, maybe they'll think that you're on the phone, or laughing at something funny on TV. But laugh out loud for 60 seconds. Force yourself to do it, and I'm telling you, moments into it, you're going to start actually laughing uncontrollably, and if there's anyone else around, they're going to join you and be laughing too.

Have FUN with this! Enjoy this day. Enjoy your laughter.

One Minute of Laughter

RECAP YOUR DAY

Did you do the challenge?

What happened?

How was the experience?

"A Better TODAY"

Day 8

Extra Time in Bed

We are on Day 8 of The 30 Day Challenge on How to Have a Better TODAY. I hope you enjoyed the first week. It was a lot of fun!

For Day 8, it might be a little too late for this today, so you might have to do this tomorrow, or do it tonight. What I'd like you to do is spend five extra minutes in bed.

Sounds hard, right? Challenging, right? I'm being humorous here.

The reason I want you to do that is when you're spending that extra five minutes in bed, I just want you to be shut off from all electronics. Try and just relax your mind, and lie there in appreciation of your bed, your pillow, the blankets, your body, how it feels. Appreciate and marinate in how good it feels to be able to sleep in a bed like that.

How lucky you are to sleep in a bed! Do you know how many people in this world never know that luxury? It's crazy.

It's a simple thing, but it's that level of appreciation of all the little gifts in our lives that allow us to see more gifts in everything else and live intentionally, in appreciation, in gratitude every single day.

That is your challenge for TODAY…just spend five extra minutes in bed in gratitude and appreciation.

RECAP YOUR DAY

Did you do the challenge?

What happened?

How was the experience?

"A Better TODAY"

Day 9

A Little Decadence

It's Day 9 of The 30 Day Challenge on How to Have a Better TODAY.

To recap Day 8, what I asked you to do was just spend five extra minutes in bed, just appreciating it. Appreciating the bed, appreciating your thoughts, the quiet, your body. Just experience it and understand what a gift that bed that you get to sleep in every night is. That was yesterday's challenge.

Today, the challenge is, I want you to do something decadent for yourself. I want you to buy something decadent or do something decadent for yourself.

Decadent might be having an ice cream cone. Decadent might be taking a bath. Decadent might be buying a new lipstick or a new scarf or something. Just one little thing that you would consider "decadent" for yourself. Just treat yourself to one little thing today. Something that's FUN!

What I want you to do when you do this is have ZERO guilt associated with it. Do not feel bad about pampering you! I want you to nurture yourself that way and treat yourself that way.

You're extraordinary and you deserve it!

Don't beat yourself up over it. Don't feel like, "I should be using this money for something else, to pay a bill or to give to somebody else," or to do anything other than taking care of yourself with it.

That's my challenge to you today. Simple, easy stuff, right? Do something, buy something decadent just for YOU!

A Little Decadence

RECAP YOUR DAY

Did you do the challenge?

What happened?

How was the experience?

"A Better TODAY"

Day 10

An Unplanned Getaway

**Hi there, it's Diane Forster with Day 10 of The 30 Day Challenge on How to Have a Better TODAY.
How exciting!**

Okay, Day 8, what I asked you to do was to stay in bed five extra minutes.

Day 9, I said to do or buy something decadent just for you.

Today on Day 10, what I'm going to ask you to do is take out your calendar, and I want you to put an unplanned vacation or getaway on your calendar. Just pick some day in the not-too-distant future and mark it on your calendar that you are taking a vacation. You don't have to fill in where you're going yet or what you're doing yet but block off that time.

Now, once you have that time blocked off, now you're going to work it backwards. It's like reverse engineering. Some of us think, you know, we just don't have the time to go places and do things. We don't have the money to do it, and we just let the days, the weeks, the months, the YEARS go by without traveling and doing the things that we want to do in life!

Sometimes, it could be as simple as going away close, even just two hours away from where you live is a great getaway for you! That is something that we need to be more cognizant of and make time for.

How do you do it? How to get ahead of it? Here's how: you don't save the money so that you can then go away. Put it on the calendar FIRST and then work backwards, so you are then saving towards it. Start planning it and figuring out, like, how much money do I need to go on that trip and to do that "thing" I want to do? Then, you work it backwards so you can start saving for it. Create a little account for it, whether it's at home or at the bank, but a separate place where you can put the money aside for that getaway or that dream vacation. But first, I want you to put it on the calendar.

I don't want you to wait a year from now. Maybe it's a few months from now, but don't put it SO far out in the future. Do it sooner rather than later but get it on the calendar first.

Block off that time and then reverse engineer it and you'll be amazed at how quickly that trip comes together for you...the money for it, the resources, the travel plans, whatever it is you need to make that trip happen. It'll just sort of all come together because you'll manifest it because you already put it on the calendar first.

That's my challenge to you today. Put an unplanned vacation or get away on the calendar.

RECAP YOUR DAY

Did you do the challenge?

What happened?

How was the experience?

"A Better TODAY"

Day 11

The Power of the "Calm Alarm"

Here we are on day 11 of The 30 Day Challenge on How to Have a Better TODAY. I hope you're having a good time!

I'm going to recap what we've done so far in our second week of this challenge.

Day 8, the first thing I asked you to do was just spend five extra minutes in bed.

Day 9, I said to do something or buy something that's decadent just for you. It didn't have to be big.

Day 10, I said put an unplanned vacation or getaway on your calendar and then reverse engineer it back so that you get all the savings for it, the resources for it, and let it come together. But, put it on the calendar first.

Day 11…this is what I want you to do. I want you to set what I call "Calm Alarm." Actually, title it "Calm Alarm" on your phone two times a day. I do it at 3 o'clock in the afternoon and then I do it again at 7 o'clock at night.

I picked out a pretty ring tone for it. It's very relaxing, and what happens is when that alarm goes off, it doesn't matter what I'm doing, I stop for a minute, (sometimes two) and I just close my eyes, breathe and relax. When we close our eyes, even doing nothing more than just closing our eyes, our brains go into "shutdown" mode, and we really relax and stop all the millions, literally millions, of thoughts that go on in our minds throughout the day. Doing that brief technique will just sort of reset you. It is literally a "mind minute" for yourself that you're going to do twice a day.

It is really going to have a positive impact on you. Whatever is going on, wherever you are, be sure to set two times that work for you but take two minutes out of your day and set a "Calm Alarm." Nurture yourself by giving yourself quiet…just for a MINUTE. Just sit in the quiet.

This is great for people who can't meditate and don't know how to meditate. You're actually going to be meditating in that one single minute that you set for two times a day.

That's our Challenge on Day 11…set yourself a calm alarm twice a day.

The Power of the "Calm Alarm"

RECAP YOUR DAY

Did you do the challenge?

What happened?

How was the experience?

"A Better TODAY"

Day 12

A Taste of Something New

It's Day 12 of The 30 Day Challenge on How to Have a Better TODAY.

We are in week two now, so let me recap the week so far.

Day 8, we started out by spending five extra minutes in bed.

Day 9, we bought something or did something decadent for ourselves.

Day 10, we put on an unplanned vacation on our calendar, and then you're going to reverse engineer it.

Day 11, we set a calm alarm for one minute, twice a day. Pick the times that work for you, just to close your eyes and mentally shut down.

Okay. Day 12, what we're going to do today is…I want you to eat something new that you have never eaten before.

Do you ever go to the grocery store, and you see in the produce aisle with rows of things that you don't even know what they are? There are so many things out there, so many wild, crazy, fun, exotic foods.

What I want to ask you to do today is just try SOMETHING. Try something new that you've never eaten before. It doesn't have to be something that you cook. You could go out to eat and order something that you've never tried before. Eat something new. Expand your palate. Literally expand your palate by trying a new flavor of something. Get out of the rut and the routine of always eating the same thing and just try one new thing and see if you like it or not. You may discover that this is something that you absolutely love and now you can't live without it.

My challenge to you today is to eat one new thing you've never eaten before.

A Taste of Something New

RECAP YOUR DAY

Did you do the challenge?

What happened?

How was the experience?

"A Better TODAY"

Day 13

A Road Never Traveled

We are on Day 13 of The 30 Day Challenge on How to Have a Better TODAY. I hope you're enjoying this because I sure am.

Let me recap the week because I'm recapping each week as we go along.

Day 8, we started with spending five extra minutes in bed.

Then on Day 9, we bought something that was decadent for ourselves.

Day 10, we put an unplanned vacation on the calendar. We're going to reverse engineer and save for it. We're going to go the opposite way.

Day 11, we set a calm alarm for ourselves twice a day, one minute, just to shut down.

Then on Day 12, we ate something new. We tried some new food that we had never eaten before.

So, Day 13, what I want you to do today is, I want you to take a different route today. If that's commuting to work, taking your kids to school, running errands, going to visit your mom or your grandmother or whatever it is you're doing today. I want you to take a different route.

Go a different way. Observe the homes, the trees, the stores, the community. Anything and everything that you can by taking a different route.

The purpose is we're just trying to break the habits that we have. We get in ruts and routines. We sleep on the same side of the bed. We get out of bed the same way. We brush our teeth with the same hand. We take the same route to work.

Whatever we do, we get sort of "robotic" with it and so we just want to shake it up a little bit.

I want you to take a different route today. Go look at something, observe something different that you have not seen before. A road you've never traveled would be my suggestion. So, that's it. Simple and easy, like everything else. You can hardly call these things challenges. They're really kind of fun.

That's the challenge for you today is to take a different route. Have fun and enjoy the scenery.

RECAP YOUR DAY

Did you do the challenge?

_____
_____
_____
_____

What happened?

_____
_____
_____
_____

How was the experience?

_____
_____
_____
_____

"A Better TODAY"

Day 14

A Dozen Achieved Goals

We're two weeks into this, almost at the halfway point, and I hope you're getting a lot of benefit from this. I'm having so much fun with it!

Let's recap before we give you today's challenge. Here's what we've done this week so far.

Day 8 was to spend five extra minutes in bed. Challenge, right? Stay in bed.

Day 9 was to do something decadent for yourself.

Day 10 was to put an unplanned vacation on your calendar and then reverse engineer it.

Day 11 was the calm alarm. Set the calm alarm twice during the day just to shut down your mind and shut everything down for 60 seconds, two times a day.

Day 12 was to eat something new that you had never eaten before; either prepared at home or out somewhere but stretch your palate.

Day 13 was to take a different route to school or work, or wherever you go.

Travel a road you haven't traveled before.

Day 14… I would say from everything that I've given you so far, today is probably the biggest "challenge" out of all of them. What I'd like you to do is get out your calendar, and I want you to put in one goal per month for an entire year. Maybe the objective is at the end of the year, you have achieved one massive goal. Or it could be 12 different things that you've done throughout the year.

Let me give you an example of a big goal. One massive goal might be that you would like to lose a lot of weight. Let's just throw out 50 pounds. Say you're someone who wants to lose 50 pounds, but when you think about that up front, it is overwhelming and daunting. You probably tried a million diets and anything and everything under the sun. It's depressing, I get it, because it's just too daunting to get over it that way. But let's break it out over a year.

What I want you to do first is IMAGINE yourself 50 pounds lighter one year from today. Just kind of sit in that and marinate in it for as long as possible…several minutes if you can…on how good that feels. Right? If you break out 50 pounds over the course of a year, that translates to 4 or 5 pounds a month, which translates to about A POUND A WEEK! When you break it out like that, not so daunting, right? Much better to do it that way!!!

Put it on your calendar, whatever it is. It might be that you want to get in a romantic relationship. You'd like to be in love and married a year from now. Or you'd like to switch careers and be in a new industry a year from now. Whatever your goal is, put it down.

I'm going to reference James Altucher's book "Choose Yourself." I'm going to reference this book a lot, because there's so many good nuggets in it. What he says in this book is do 1% better a day, 1%. If you think about doing things 1% better, think of all the percentages that add up to over the course of time, over the course of weeks and months and years! It makes everything so much less daunting and a lot more achievable, easier and lighter.

That's my goal and my challenge for you today, is to put a goal on the calendar each month for an entire year. Whether it's one or it's a collection of goals.

A Dozen Achieved Goals

RECAP YOUR DAY

Did you do the challenge?

___

What happened?

___

How was the experience?

___

"A Better TODAY"

Day 15

A Tiny Task to Tidy Up

We are on Day 15 of The 30 Day Challenge on How to Have a Better TODAY.

Today's challenge is pretty simple. It shouldn't take you that long to do. What I'm going to ask you to do is clean out one drawer...one drawer that is frustrating you. Maybe it's your sock drawer. Maybe it's your junk drawer. Maybe it's a filing drawer, but just pick one of them. All I'm asking you to do is just clean out one.

What happens is clutter in our world is clutter in our minds, and it really distracts us and takes away our focus from us.

Do you ever do this? If you don't do this, I highly recommend that you do this challenge today because it does feel really good.

When I clean out a junk drawer, I feel better! (I don't have a lot of them. If you could see my home, I'm extremely neat. In fact, I'm pretty anal. My sisters call me "Di-anal." Please don't call me that!) But I do have my drawers and my spaces that are cluttered and messy. When I take the time...sometimes I'm looking for something and it stops me because I can't find it, I'm frustrated, digging through a drawer...I'll just stop and take the 10, 15, 20 minutes, 30 minutes, whatever it is and clean out that drawer and get it all organized. Then, I end up finding other things that I've been looking for!

It just makes you feel better. It makes you feel lighter. It makes you feel like you've accomplished something, which is always a great feeling. My challenge for you today is just clean out one drawer, just declutter one drawer.

That's all I'm giving you today, very simple and easy like everything else.

A Tiny Task to Tidy Up

RECAP YOUR DAY

Did you do the challenge?

What happened?

How was the experience?

"A Better TODAY"

Day 16

Music to Move You

We are continuing The 30 Day Challenge on How to Have a Better TODAY. Today is day 16.

Yesterday, on Day 15, I asked you to clean out one drawer. Just take a few minutes, pick a drawer, just one, and clean it out and declutter it and find things you've known have been missing. More importantly, it gives you a sense of accomplishment, like you've done something. It just makes you feel good and lifts your spirit.

Today, what I want you to do is, if you don't have one, I am encouraging you to pick a "theme song." Play this song every day. Have it be something that is uplifting and puts you in a good mood. It's a great way to start the day.

It might be something that you already listen to. Maybe you could purchase the ringtone for it and set it as your alarm, so that's what gets you going first thing in the morning. Listen to it while you're working out, or going for a walk, or you're commuting. But pick a theme song.

For me, I don't know why, lately I'm into KC and the Sunshine Band. I'm very retro, I guess! I read a comment from one of my video posts, and someone had written that she loves my videos and "keep them coming." As soon as I read those words, "keep them coming," KC and the Sunshine's song, "Keep it Coming, Love" started playing in my head and then, I started bouncing to the beat.

I am now using that as my morning theme song. I've picked other songs in the past that are just fun and upbeat, and they just make me feel good. Right now, I listen to that song every day. Once a day. I will listen to it until I get tired of it and then, I'll pick a different one. It's always something that's fun and upbeat.

That's my challenge for you, is to pick a fun song as your theme song and listen to it every day. Have it lift your spirit.

RECAP YOUR DAY

Did you do the challenge?

What happened?

How was the experience?

"A Better TODAY"

Day 17

Don't "Should" All Over Yourself

We are back with Day 17 of The 30 Day Challenge on How to Have a Better TODAY.

Day 15, I asked you to clean out one drawer, just for a sense of accomplishment.

Day 16, I asked you to pick out a fun theme song to start your day, and to maybe set it as your alarm tone in the morning or listen to it first thing, perhaps when you're working out, going for a walk, commuting or whatever it is.

Today, what I want you to do is be aware if you use the phrase, "You should," when you're talking to people. "You should…da, da, da…" If you don't say it, become aware if people say it to you and the effect it has on you.

That is an expression that I used to hear a lot in my life, and I think I might have even said it a lot. I've really worked hard to get that out of my vocabulary when I'm communicating with other people, because frankly, I shouldn't be telling anyone what they should be doing. Unless they're specifically asking me for my advice on something, I will be honest with them and give them my honest opinion. Otherwise, "You should do something" without an invitation for some advice, is really off-putting to some people.

I'm not even saying that you do this or not. I just want you to be aware if this is something that you do. If so, just try and understand that it might not be the best way to communicate with somebody, because it implies to them, what they hear and how they receive it, is that there's something wrong with them. You know what? There's nothing wrong with any of us.

It's just one of those things, and I don't want to phrase it to you like, "You should be aware if you say, 'You should.'" That's not what I'm saying. I'm just saying it in a way to just be cognizant if that's an expression that you use. And if it's not, if someone else uses it with you, how it makes you feel.

That's today's challenge. Just be aware of those two words together as a directive to somebody when it's unsolicited or uninvited. It's probably not coming off the way you want it to.

That's it, just simple awareness. Make it an amazing day.

RECAP YOUR DAY

Did you do the challenge?

What happened?

How was the experience?

"A Better TODAY"

Day 18

One Thing for Another

It's Day 18 of The 30 Day Challenge on How to Have a Better TODAY.

Day 15 was cleaning out one drawer. Declutter it so that you can feel like you've accomplished something.

Day 16 was picking an upbeat theme song to boost your mood first thing in the day, as soon as you start the day.

Day 17 was to be aware of the usage of the phrase "You should" to somebody in an unsolicited environment.

Day 18…this one's actually heavy, and this one is going to be a challenge. Now, before I tell you what it is I want to preface this by saying that this series is all about YOU, and yeah, I'm having a lot of fun with it with the laughter and all of that stuff. But there are some serious challenges here as well. I think if you're here, it's because there's something that you want to look at too, but I want you to know this is ALWAYS a "no judgment" zone. You don't have to share this with anybody. This is all about you, your well-being, and you living the most fulfilling, intentional life each day that you can.

That said, let me tell you what it is. What I'd like you to do is, if you can, eliminate or at least mitigate your use or habit of something that does not make you feel good and is not serving you. Say you're a smoker, or you drink too much alcohol, or you have bad eating habits, or you're addicted to porn, or you drink too much Coke, or you snort too much coke, or you take sleeping pills, or you're addicted to prescription drugs. Whatever it is, it really doesn't matter. It could be something as benign as you drink too much coffee.

Whatever the scenario is, I'd like you today to eliminate it or mitigate it.

I don't believe in deprivation. This is a rich, fulfilling, abundant universe, so I don't like to say words like deprivation. Therefore, what you could do is REPLACE that habit with something else.

Instead of just removing it, replace it with something else and think about this for a while... I really want you to spend this day pondering this for you if there's something in your life that you really don't want to be doing anymore and you want to break the habit. You know there are resources out there for help, and I don't want this to be a daunting task for you. I want you to know that YOU have the power to CHOOSE. You alone could make yourself do or not do anything as long as you BELIEVE in it.

I know this was a little bit heavier today, but I would like you to look at what it is that you would like to eliminate or mitigate in your life and replace that habit instead of removing it. Good luck with this challenge. I am always here for you, by the way. Feel free to reach out and comment to me. I keep a confidentiality agreement with all my clients and the same applies to you, so I am here if you ever need me, and trust me that whatever it is, your secret is safe with me. Okay?

RECAP YOUR DAY

Did you do the challenge?

What happened?

How was the experience?

"A Better TODAY"

Day 19

What's Your Wish, Wish, Wish

We are on Day 19 of our 30 day challenge on how to have a better today.

Day 15, we started with cleaning out one drawer. Declutter it so you feel a sense of accomplishment.

Day 16, I asked you to pick out a fun upbeat theme song as your way to start your day.

Day 17, I said be aware of your use of the phrase, "You should," if it's unsolicited.

Then Day 18 was a heavy one. I wanted you to try to eliminate or mitigate a bad habit that you have that you think you have and try to replace it with something else versus remove something.

Okay, Day 19, this is back to being fun. What I want you to do is I want you to write down three wishes. A wish, a goal, a dream. Just like Aladdin's lamp with three wishes, write down your three. It could be related to relationships, family, health, career, money… ANYTHING that you want it to be about that you'd like to manifest and attract into your life.

What I want you to do is when you write down these three things, I want you to add a "by when" date. For instance, say you're single. You've never been married, and that's something that you'd like to attract into your life and manifest. An example would be to just say, "I set the intention to invite my spouse into my life and that we fall in love, and we're married by June 30th."

Something like that…now you get the gist of it.

What I want you to do is pick three things that you would like to attract and manifest into your life. Put the "by when" date. Then, I want you to fold this piece of paper up and I want you to put it away. Put it away somewhere where you won't find it easily. Like Ron Popeil used to say, "Set it and forget it." I want you to set it somewhere and forget about it.

Don't even keep it conscious in your mind. What you do next is put a date on the calendar in about a year from now to search for and find that piece of paper. You can then see when these goals came into your life because, trust me, they ARE coming into your life!

If you do this and you believe in it, you set it and forget it, and then just let it go and let the universe go to work on it, you're going to attract these things into your life! This is so much fun! I am a magical, magnetic manifestor. We ALL are, I'm just highly acutely aware of my manifestation skills. I love it when I see other people manifesting into their lives. It doesn't get any more fun than that!

That's my challenge for you today. I can't wait to hear what things you manifested into your life, so just have FUN with it!

RECAP YOUR DAY

Did you do the challenge?

What happened?

How was the experience?

"A Better TODAY"

Day 20

Make Learning a Priority

We're back with Day 20 of The 30 Day Challenge. We're two-thirds of the way through it already. Wow! I hope you are enjoying this because I truly am enjoying doing this for you!

Let's recap this week so far.

Day 15 was to clean out one drawer.

Day 16 was picking a theme song. Pick out a fun upbeat theme song.

Day 17 was watching your use of the words, "you should." Day 18 was to eliminate or mitigate a habit that you have in your life that you want to replace with something else that is healthier or better for you.

Day 19 was writing a list of three goals, wishes, and dreams that you want to manifest into your life with a "by when" date.

Today's challenge is I want you to sign up for a class. Do something new, something different. This doesn't have to be a 12-week course, or anything that's long term. This could be a one-time only Salsa dancing class, or a cooking class or race car driving class… but pick something.

Sign up and do something different that you've wanted to do.

The reason why is that the learning never stops. We are students of life, and there's always room, there's always time, and there's always the money to continue learning and growing and doing. It just takes COMMITMENT, and it takes ACTION. It takes self-discipline to actually commit yourself to doing it.

I'm giving you this opportunity to take advantage of something that you've wanted to do. You know what it is. I don't know what it is. I can't tell you what it is for you.

We can say those excuses to ourselves, all day, every day. I've said them before. Then, the days, the weeks, the months, the years, go by and all that time lapses and we haven't done the things that we wanted to do. We need to make the time and the commitment to doing it.

Sign up for a new class today. It could be a hot yoga class if you've never done that. That's something that I'm going to do actually because, I haven't done that, and I do want to do that. I'm going to sign up and see if I like it.

That is your challenge today, sign up for a new class and continue learning. Be a student of life and have an amazing day.

Make Learning a Priority

RECAP YOUR DAY

Did you do the challenge?

What happened?

How was the experience?

"A Better TODAY"

Day 21

You Are a Magnet

It's Day 21 of The 30 Day Challenge on How to Have a Better TODAY.

Let me recap our full week.

Day 15 we started cleaning out one drawer.

Day 16 we added a theme song, an upbeat theme song into our lives.

Day 17 we became aware of the use of the phrase "you should" in our lives.

Day 18 was heavy. That was the day all about eliminating or mitigating a bad habit out of our lives and replacing that with a new one and knowing that we have the power to choose. We need to decide every day how we want to live.

Day 19 was to write down three of the goals, wishes, desires, things that you want to manifest into your life with a "by when" date.

Then Day 20 was to sign up for one new class, whether it be a one-time only class or something new that you wanted to do. Just make the commitment, take the action and do it. Include it into your life because it's something that you want to do. It's going to lift you up and make you feel so much better by doing it.

Okay, Day 21. I want you to write this down and put this somewhere where you can see this every day of your life. For years, I had it taped to my computer keyboard area so that I would see it and I would say it aloud every day. I use this mantra all the time. You ready? Write this down.

"I am a magnet for love, money, success, and happiness."

I'll repeat it.

"I am a magnet for love, money, success, and happiness."

I choose those four words for a reason.

Love for obvious reasons. Love, in every way, shape, form…I want to be a magnet for and invite that into my life.

Money…not for greedy reasons, but we all need to make a living. Right? We all need money to come into our lives. I want to be a magnet for it. I want to attract it to come into my life easily and effortlessly.

Success because success is for me, and I hope for a lot of people, isn't defined by my net worth or anything like that. Success is defined on how I want to FEEL in my life, every day. Every day I want to feel like a success. Who wants to feel like a failure? Success is much more about a feeling.

Then, happiness is the ultimate goal. Don't we all want to be happy?

I chose those four words intentionally. I say that mantra every single day. I am a magnet for love, money, success, and happiness. I write it in my journal often, and I say it and think it a lot. I want to impart that and give that to you because I think that mantra serves everybody really well.

That's my challenge for you today, to write that down and put it somewhere where you can see it every day and get in the habit of saying it.

RECAP YOUR DAY

Did you do the challenge?

What happened?

How was the experience?

"A Better TODAY"

Day 22

You Aren't Your Story

It's Day 22 of The 30 Day Challenge on How to Have a Better TODAY.

This is the start of the fourth week, and it will actually go four and a half weeks. We are rounding towards the end.

Today, the challenge for you is this…

I want you to stop telling your story and change it. If there's something from your past that you're carrying around with you, someone did you wrong or hurt you, or harmed you, or you're putting blame on somebody else for something about your past, anyone else, let it go. It could be the government, it could be your family, it could be anybody in your life… a former boss, a boyfriend or a girlfriend, or spouse, or anything from your past that is a story that you're still telling…YOU are the only one that's keeping it alive unfortunately. I hate to tell you that, but it's in the past where it belongs. NOTHING you want is back there. Everything that you want is in FRONT of you!

I'm encouraging you to change your story. Just tell a different story. Put a different spin on it. I practice this a lot and it took me a while to get to this, but I will tell you, when you're no longer telling that sad, sob story and you're finding the gift in whatever it was and looking for the positive outcome in whatever it was, it really changes the trajectory of your life in such a powerful, positive way!

The truth is, and I know I say that a lot, but the truth is that you just don't want to be living in your past. Your life is TODAY. It's right NOW, and the best way to start living today intentionally, on purpose, is to stop living in your past. The quickest way to stop living in your past is to stop telling your story.

Change it. Don't make that story be who you are. That does not define who you are. You are no longer that person. That person no longer exists. Whatever happened to you no longer exists. It's our ability to hang onto it and our repetition of the story that is the only thing that keeps it alive.

Today, and each day going forward, change your story. Stop telling the old one and change it up. That's my challenge for you today.

RECAP YOUR DAY

Did you do the challenge?

_____
_____
_____
_____

What happened?

_____
_____
_____
_____

How was the experience?

_____
_____
_____
_____

"A Better TODAY"

Day 23

Thirsty for Water

It's Day 23 of The 30 Day Challenge on How to Have a Better TODAY.

Yesterday on Day 22, the challenge was to stop telling your old story, to change it up and make a new one because you do not want to be living in your past, and you're the only one keeping it alive.

Today, my challenge for you is this, very simple. See if you can drink water only. For one whole day. Just water. No coffee, no soda pop, no alcohol, nothing else, just water for one whole day. Hydrate yourself as much as you possibly can.

You know we're supposed to drink on average half of our body weight in ounces, so if you weigh 130 pounds, you're supposed to drink 65 ounces of water a day. I don't know how good you are about it, but I need constant reminders to make sure that I stay hydrated, so I keep water around me at all times.

I'm making it really simple today. Water is what our body needs more than anything else. Next to air, the next thing we need is water. If you know that this is something that you really need to be better about and incorporate more into your life, try to create a way to build on it and make it more of a habit for you. Try setting an alarm every hour to remind you to SIP on water. In order to stay properly hydrated, in addition to eating green leafy vegetables, when you drink water, you need to sip on it all day.

If you forget to drink the water in sips throughout the day and you're instead guzzling it and downing it, it's like pouring water on a really dry plant. You know what happens…it runs out the bottom of it and it doesn't absorb it. Well, the same thing happens with our body.

In order to stay properly hydrated, we need to be drinking water, sipping on water all day long. So, my challenge for you today is just to drink only water today, for all of your liquid intake today. See if you can do it.

Thirsty for Water

RECAP YOUR DAY

Did you do the challenge?

What happened?

How was the experience?

"A Better TODAY"

Day 24

Plant Power

I'm back with Day 24 of The 30 Day Challenge.

Day 22, the challenge was to stop telling your old story and change it to a new one.

Day 23, I asked you to drink water only all day long. Have that be your only source of liquid intake for one day.

Day 24, what I'm going to ask you to do is buy a plant or, if you have them around, keep a plant near you as much as possible. Preferably near a window or door where it can get sunlight. Plant life has such healing effects and benefits on us.

Think about what a plant does besides being beautiful and providing us with shelter, providing us with food, providing us with oxygen. It's a whole yin yang thing that we do with our plants. It's not just for the outdoors; it's for the indoors, too.

We know everything is energy. I talk about this all the time.

Plants also talk to you and speak to you. You may think this sounds crazy, but if you have something that's bothering you or a question about something and you want to know what the answer is, our souls know everything, and plants can communicate with us directly on an inner-soul level. It's amazing. It is true.

If there's something that's bothering me or some issue that I have a question about, what I'll do is I'll hold the leaf of the plant and I'll actually ask the question aloud. I'll get a sensation in my body. We have three minds: our head, our heart, our gut. I'll get it somewhere in either of those three places, the head, the heart, or the gut, and it'll feel good, or it'll feed bad. That is a yes or a no. Every time I do this, I get an answer. It's always the right answer, so I like to have a plant around me whenever possible. Let's face it, what greater insight is there than that?

This was a little trick I learned at a workshop that I attended about a year ago, and I've implemented this and use this practice a lot. It works for me. I hope it works for you.

My challenge for you today (it's so easy, it's hardly a challenge to call this series a challenge) is to find a plant in your house or go out and buy one and keep it near you as much as you possibly can. Okay?

RECAP YOUR DAY

Did you do the challenge?

What happened?

How was the experience?

"A Better TODAY"

Day 25

The Present of Presence

It's Day 25 of The 30 Day Challenge on How to Have a Better TODAY.

Day 22, I asked you to stop telling your old story and to change it up and make a new one.

Day 23, I asked you to drink water as your only source of liquid all day long.

Day 24, I asked you to keep a plant nearby and enjoy all the benefits of having a living plant near you for not only the oxygen it provides, but also for the guidance it provides.

Today, Day 25, I'm going to ask you to do this: Be present as much as you possibly can all day today.

Try not to think about the past. Try not to think about the future. Be present today. I know that's hard. Our minds tend to want to go back, or they want to go forward, but really live as intentionally and present as you can today. I'm going to tell you a couple of tricks that I do sometimes that help me make it work.

I wear a plain rubber band. You could do this with a bracelet, but you don't even need jewelry. I'll put a little rubber band around my wrist as a reminder for me to stay present. When I see it, I remember? You can flip it from wrist to wrist if you catch yourself not doing it but then back to the other wrist when you find that you are living in the present moment again.

Another trick I learned from a really good friend of mine is ... I draw a little gift box on the inside of my wrist/arm area. I draw an actual "present." Sometimes I need a little reminder. I'm not encouraging you to doodle on yourself, but I'm just saying this is a really effective trick without actually having a tattoo. I have a temporary reminder to stay present and be present. Seems silly, right?

Your life is RIGHT NOW. Listen, I preach this all the time.

I HAVE TODAY! The company name says it all. The poem says it all. I'm an Intentional Living Expert. I write all my blogs on intentional living. Intentional Living means being present in each moment.

I do my very best to capture the essence of every single moment… to really FEEL my life, every minute of my life; the good, the bad, the ugly, the beautiful, all of it. To be present for all of it because our lives are now, now, now, now, now. Do you ever notice that tomorrow never comes, because when tomorrow comes, it's today? It's NOW.

My challenge for you today is to try and remember that and be as present as you possibly can. I would love your feedback. Let me know what sort of tricks you come up with that are reminders that help you to stay living your life in the present moment and living it intentionally.

RECAP YOUR DAY

Did you do the challenge?

What happened?

How was the experience?

"A Better TODAY"

Day 26

Judgement Day...Not

Can you believe it's Day 26 of The 30 Day Challenge on How to Have a Better TODAY?

Let me recap the week so far.

Day 22 was to stop telling your old story, to change it and make a new one.

Day 23 was to only drink water all day long.

Day 24 was to keep a living plant near you as much as possible.

Day 25 was to be as present as you possibly can all day long.

It's Day 26. No judgement. Do your best to live without judgement of anyone or anything.

We live in this beautiful, diverse world. It's what makes it so colorful and flavorful and unique is the fact that every single person is different. There are no two people who are exactly alike. We need to live in a world where we embrace our uniqueness and our diversity.

Imagine if we lived in a world where everybody thought the same thing, felt the same way, practiced the same religion, liked the same food, wore the same clothes, and thought the same way about politics. I mean, what a boring world that would be.

It's not our place to judge anybody by what they do, by what they think, by what they look like, how they sound. None of it is our right to judge. It's simply to love and accept unconditionally.

It's a challenge, I know! We were raised with those old paradigms. There's outside influences all around us, but we have to remember that we all deserve to be here.

We all have every right to be here. We all have every right to feel the way we feel and think the way we think and do what we want to do. Within reason. We do not want to harm anybody else. Live today and each day going forward without judgement.

The goal of this 30 Day Challenge is that I'm giving you little things to do and to become aware of, but they're all building upon each other.

I do the same, momentum-building processes in my book, "I Have Today" as well as my other fun, powerful programs that are listed at the end of this book. When you make small, subtle changes like this, and you "recap to remember", that builds momentum and leads to lasting, permanent, positive change.

The goal for today and going forward is to live without judgement. That's it. I'm making it really simple for you. I just want to create awareness of that if that lives in you.

I used to be an extremely judgmental person, and I can't even believe that I allowed myself to live like that. I didn't know as much as I know now. However, like Oprah Winfrey says, "When you know better, you do better." I do my very best to live judgment-free, and my life is so much more peaceful.

RECAP YOUR DAY

Did you do the challenge?

What happened?

How was the experience?

"A Better TODAY"

Day 27

Worthy Words

I'm here with Day 27 of The 30 Day Challenge on How to Have a Better TODAY. I hope you're enjoying this because I really am! I love doing this!

I'm going to make today's challenge a little bit lighter than yesterday. Yesterday was a little bit heavier but let me recap so far this week.

Day 22 was to stop telling your story, your old story, and change it up.

Day 23 was to drink water as your only fluid intake for one day, just water only.

Day 24 was to keep a living plant near you.

Day 25 was to be present all day every day; to really live your life in the present moment.

Day 26 was to live with no judgment.

Day 27 is more fun. I want you to think about your favorite word. I don't know if you have ever given this any thought or if you have a lot of favorite words. I know I have a lot of words that I like, but my favorite word is "surrender." Surrender. It sounds like a negative word. It sounds weak and like giving up.

Surrender is actually a really powerful word, and it's my favorite, favorite word.

There's a Sanskrit word, "Pranidhana" which basically means when you fully give in, allow and open yourself up, the universe floods their gifts upon you, and you become one with source. That's loosely translated, but the English version of that is the word "surrender."

Sometimes if something is a struggle for me, like I'm bucking my own current with something, then I know that I'm not supposed to be doing it. So, I stop, and I literally say, "I surrender." I throw my hands up to God, the universe, Jesus, whatever you believe in, and say, "You take over. I'm giving this to you. I surrender to you." Then, whatever it is always works out the way it's supposed to. It always turns out to be okay. Usually better than okay…better than I thought it was going to be.

I love that word. Surrender is a powerful word. I just love it. There are many other words that I like, but that is my favorite word.

My challenge for you today is to figure out what your favorite word is, and then think about why it is your favorite word. What's the meaning behind it for you? I would love to hear your words, so send me your comments, send me your favorite words and let me know why they are.

RECAP YOUR DAY

Did you do the challenge?

What happened?

How was the experience?

"A Better TODAY"

Day 28

Decide to Decide

We are on Day 28 of The 30 Day Challenge on How to Have a Better TODAY!

Let me recap the week so far.

Day 22, if you'll remember it was to stop telling your old story. Change it up. Make it better.

Day 23 was to drink water all day long. Water only, no other liquids. Just water.

Day 24 was to keep a plant by you, near you, and benefit from all the healing elements of doing that.

Day 25 was to be present as much as possible.

Day 26 was trying to live without judgement as much as you possibly can.

Day 27 was to figure out what is your favorite word.

Day 28 is this. Are you ready? I want you to make quick, quick decisions all day today. Try very hard not to go, "Um, uh, I don't know. Well, what do you want to do? Whatever you want."

I want you to decide. Decide, decide, decide all day today! Fire off decisions all day today. Be as decisive as you can possibly be and watch the POWER of PRODUCTIVITY that comes into your life today by being a quick decision maker.

I've been doing personal development and business development for years, but really honed in on my personal development recently.

One of the things that I found out about myself is I am a pretty decisive person. I'm a doer, I'm highly driven, and I get things done. I mean, I launched two companies at the same time. Two at the same time! Who does that? Only someone who's got decision making skills. Yet, what I found out is even as decisive as I am, I'm STILL NOT as decisive as I could be and should be and WANT to be!

So, I've really been working on my decision-making skills, and I have to tell you, it's really powerfully impacting my life. I realized there is always room for improvement. This is the thing that stalls so many people is their lack and inability to be decisive and to make decisions. You just have to decide!

There's no harm in making a mistake. You know what? If you try something and it's not right, then you try something else. The thing is, you've got to move, and you've got to decide, and the way to do that is to just make quick decisions.

That is my challenge for you today…to be quick at decision making all day.

Practice it no matter what you're doing. If you're debating whether or not to go work out, Go! Work out. If you're debating what to have for breakfast, just pick something! And on and on…do that all day today. You're going to have an amazing, impactful, powerful, productive day! I promise you, you will!

RECAP YOUR DAY

Did you do the challenge?

What happened?

How was the experience?

"A Better TODAY"

Day 29

Your Emails Can Wait

It's Day 29 of The 30 Day Challenge on How to Have a Better TODAY!

Let me recap the week so far.

Day 22, if you'll remember, we said to stop telling your old story. Change it up.

Day 23, drink only water all day long.

Day 24 was keeping a plant near you.

Day 25 was to be present as much as you possibly can.

Day 26 was to live without judgement as much as you possibly can.

Day 27 was to figure out what is your favorite word.

Day 28 was to be very quick at making decisions all day. Be very, very decisive.

Here we are on Day, 29 and what I want you to do is this… I want you to only check your emails two times today.

It's going to be a challenge. It is called a "challenge." Some things have to actually be challenging.

Maybe you want to do it at 9 or 10 in the morning, then maybe at 4 or 5 in the afternoon. But DO NOT be at the mercy of and responding to what other people's needs are.

That is the reason why I'm asking you to do this. You take CONTROL back of YOUR day. You take your time back. THAT is how you do it.

There is nothing in your emails that is so pressing that it can't wait for the window of time that you allow yourself to check. If it is something that is urgent, somebody is going to pick up the phone and call you! Or they'll send you a text. They'll reach out to you another way. But that's my challenge for you today.

What you're doing is you're taking back your time. You're in control of your time again, and you're not spending the day getting distracted. You know what I mean…you start working on something, the next thing you know you're checking emails, then it's hard to get back to focusing on what you're doing. That's why you block off two windows of time today to check your emails. Then, see how much more effective and focused you are and how you'll actually allow more time within your day for you to spend time doing what you want to do.

RECAP YOUR DAY

Did you do the challenge?

What happened?

How was the experience?

"A Better TODAY"

Day 30

Keep Your Feet on the Ground

We are on Day 30 of The 30 Day Challenge on How to Have a Better TODAY!

Thank you for sticking with me! It really means a lot to me!

I'm going to recap from Day 22 up till now. I was recapping each week, but this one is a little bit longer since I've added on the last two days.

Day 22 was to stop telling your old story, change it up and make it a new one.

Day 23 was to only drink water all day long as your form of liquid substance.

Day 24 was to keep a living plant near you.

Day 25 was to be present as much as possible.

Day 26 was to live without judgment as much as you possibly can.

Day 27 was to discover your favorite word.

Day 28 was to make quick decisions all day long as much as you possibly can.

Day 29 was to only check your emails two times a day, if possible, three at the most. But two would be ideal.

Okay, Day 30, are you ready for your last day's challenge? This is it…

Take a walk!

Go take a walk. I don't know if this is something that you do on a regular basis. If it is something you do on a regular basis, make it a little bit longer. If it's not something that you do, step outside and go for a walk. It does not matter what the weather is. Dress appropriately for the weather. Like I said earlier on in the series when I said, "take a different route to work," I want you to just notice and observe things you hadn't seen before. I want you to do the same thing with this walk.

Maybe take a road that you've never walked down before.

Or, if there's a path and a trail that you've been curious about, take the time out to go and explore it, breathe in the fresh air, and notice all the life around you. Look at things that you've never looked at before. Spend some time just staring at the sky but give yourself this gift of taking a walk.

Get yourself out of your setting and put yourself in a new natural setting and allow your body to feel the healing energy and properties of that.

If you can, do you want a bonus to this? If you're in a place where there's grass and it's not winter where there's snow on the ground or it's cold, take off your shoes and socks and put your bare feet on the earth. Let the electromagnetic energy of the earth come up through your feet and heal your body. It's called "Grounding," and it is so powerfully healing!

My 30th Day Challenge for you is so simple. I mean, it's hardly a challenge, but give yourself the GIFT of taking a walk.

RECAP YOUR DAY

Did you do the challenge?

What happened?

How was the experience?

In Gratitude

Now that we did this 30 Day series together, I want to Thank You from the bottom of my heart for taking this journey with me! I hope you had SO much fun!

Like I said at the beginning of this and in the middle of it, it's these little subtle things that allow us to live each day intentionally and more on purpose with more joy, with more fulfillment, with more happiness.

There's definitely more AWARENESS, and it really does add to the richness of your life.

I have loved, loved, loved doing this book for you.

It is my mission in life to be here for you, and I look forward to seeing you soon. Share your stories with me…I LOVE hearing them! What was your favorite challenge? Your most difficult challenge? Let me know the things that you want and how this is impacting your life, because that moves me like you can't believe.

Thank you for taking this journey with me. I love you so much.
With Love,
Diane

Now What?

I have a special invitation for you.

If you want more things like this from me, including some free gifts, be sure to go to my website at www.DianeForster.com and DianeForsterGifts.com.

Follow me on social media:
Facebook: www.facebook.com/DianeForsterOfficial
Instagram: @DianeForsterOfficial

"A BETTER TODAY" CHALLENGE

30 DAYS OF INSPIRATION & MOTIVATION

For the video version of this book, register at www.abettertodaychallenge.com.

Check out some of my amazing courses!

www.10daypassionandpurpose.com

10 Days to Your Passion and Purpose with Diane Forster

www.mindsetandmanifestationchallenge.com

MINDSET & MANIFESTATION 6 DAY CHALLENGE

THE BLUEPRINT to Quickly and Easily Take Your Ideas, Dreams and Goals from Vision to Reality So You Can Start Living Life on Your Terms!

www.haveitalllifeprogram.com

HAVE IT ALL LIFE PROGRAM

About the Author

So many women stay stuck in a life of mediocrity because they're afraid to take a leap of faith and go after the life they really want…constrained by the shackles of what society has told them they should be happy with, feelings of unworthiness, and the fears associated with making change. The number one age group for suicide attempts are women 45-64. This time of life is full of transitions and major life changes, and many women suffer from feelings of low self-worth and value. Whether it's becoming an empty nester, going through divorce, feeling stuck in a career, many women in this age group feel hopeless and lost.

Feeling stuck in her own life in a career that was no longer fulfilling and a marriage that left her feeling empty and alone, Diane hit a breaking point that almost ended her life. After experiencing a miracle during her suicide attempt, Diane was determined to figure a way out of that life, and she discovered that all the pain and suffering was a direct result of what her mindset and limiting beliefs were leading her to believe was true. Once she was aware of what had been happening, she discovered the path and the processes out of that life to be able to step into the extraordinary life she now lives.

As a powerful Life and Mindset Coach and leader in her industry, Diane guides women through a transformation on how to release the limiting beliefs and negative self-talk that hold them back (a.k.a. the dandelions) and open themselves up to the dreams they've kept hidden (a.k.a. their bed of roses) so that they can reinvent what's not working to, instead, live inspired, empowered, intentional lives. She is on a mission to see that 1 billion women who don't know their self-worth discover their true divinity, power, and purpose.

Diane Forster is an **_Intentional Living Expert_**, the **_2020 Life Coach of the Year in California_**, an **_award-winning inventor, TEDx Speaker_, best-selling author of "_I Have Today...Find Your Passion, Purpose and Smile...Finally!_", and the creator of the _Rapid Mindset Shift Method_ ™**, offering women over 40 life transformational results in as little as 90 days. Diane helps women reinvent their lives and leave behind a life of mediocrity so they can manifest their dreams into reality and live to their fullest potential feeling self-love and self-worth.

Diane's TV Show and podcast, **"I HAVE TODAY with Diane Forster"** offers practical, actionable steps that you can do today. She is also an award-winning inventor, author of 6 books, and has been featured on ABC, NBC, CBS, QVC, ESPN Radio, KHTS Radio, and several other TV, radio, podcasts, and magazines. She is the proud mother of twins and lives at the beach in San Diego, California.

Made in the USA
Monee, IL
06 March 2022